FAMOUS LATINOS

Frida Kahlo

Painting Her Life

Lila and Rick Guzmán

Enslow Elementary

an imprint of

Enslow Publishers, Inc.

40 Industrial Road
Box 398
Berkeley Heights, NJ 07922
USA

http://www.enslow.com

Series Adviser
Bárbara C. Cruz, Ed.D., Series Consultant
Professor, Social Science Education
University of South Florida

Series Literacy Consultant
Allan A. De Fina, Ph.D.
Past President of the New Jersey Reading Association
Professor, Department of Literacy Education
New Jersey City University

Note to Parents and Teachers: The *Famous Latinos* series supports National Council for the Social Studies (NCSS) curriculum standards. The Words to Know section introduces subject-specific vocabulary words.

This series was designed by Irasema Rivera, an award-winning Latina graphic designer.

Enslow Elementary, an imprint of Enslow Publishers, Inc.
Enslow Elementary® is a registered trademark of Enslow Publishers, Inc.

Library of Congress Cataloging-in-Publication Data

Guzmán, Lila, 1952–
    Frida Kahlo : painting her life / Lila and Rick Guzmán.– 1st ed.
        p. cm. — (Famous latinos)
    Includes index.
    ISBN 0-7660-2643-4
    1. Kahlo, Frida—Juvenile literature. 2. Painters—Mexico—Biography—
Juvenile literature. I. Kahlo, Frida. II. Guzmán, Rick. III. Title. IV. Series.
    ND259.K33G89 2006
    759.972—dc22   2005031727

Printed in the United States of America

10 9 8 7 6 5 4 3 2 1

To Our Readers: We have done our best to make sure all Internet addresses in this book were active and appropriate when we went to press. However, the author and the publisher have no control over and assume no liability for the material available on those Internet sites or on other Web sites they may link to. Any comments or suggestions can be sent by e-mail to comments@enslow.com or to the address on the back cover.

Every effort has been made to locate all copyright holders of material used in this book. If any errors or omissions have occurred, corrections will be made in future editions of this book.

❋ Contents ❋

Frida Kahlo

Frida as a child.

⁂ 1 ⁂

Frida's Childhood

Frida Kahlo was born on July 6, 1907, in Coyoacán (Ko-yo-ah-KAHN), a small village near Mexico City. She had two older sisters, Matilde and Adriana. Her sister Cristina was born a year later. Their mother, Matilde Calderón, was very strict and serious. Frida felt closer to her father, Guillermo. He worked as a photographer for the government, taking pictures of important buildings. Sometimes he took photographs of people, too. Frida went along to help with the camera. She learned how to take pictures.

Frida's father taught her about art and nature.

Guillermo, Frida's father.

Matilde,
Frida's mother.

Frida liked studying plants and animals. She thought about becoming a doctor.

When Frida was six years old, she came down with polio, a serious disease. She had to stay in bed for nine months. She finally got better, but her right leg was smaller than the left one. To make her leg stronger, Frida's father told her to play lots of sports: swimming, soccer, and bicycling.

In those days, most people did not think girls needed to go to high school. Instead, girls learned to cook and sew. Frida's father wanted her to get a good education. In 1922, when Frida was fifteen, she passed the test to get into the National

Preparatory (pree-PAIR-uh-tor-ee) School. It was the best high school in Mexico City.

The school had two thousand students, but only thirty-five of them were girls. Frida joined a group of students called "Los Cachuchas" (kah-CHOO-chas). The name means "caps." They all wore red caps. Los Cachuchas were very smart. They enjoyed reading books and talking about them. But they also liked to have fun. Sometimes they played pranks on the teachers. Once, they set off firecrackers in class. Another time, they rode a donkey down the hallway.

Sometimes Frida sneaked out of high school to explore streets like this in Mexico City.

One day a famous artist named Diego Rivera came to the school. He began painting a mural on some of the school walls. A mural is a very large painting. The Mexican government wanted murals to be painted on the walls of many public buildings. It was a great way to teach people about Mexico and its history. Diego was the most important mural painter in Mexico.

Frida often sneaked into the room to watch Diego paint. She liked to tease him, too, and even stole food from his lunch basket. But more than anything else, she liked to watch him work.

Diego worked high up on a wooden platform.

2

Learning to Paint

On September 17, 1925, Frida and her friend were on their way home from school. They jumped onto a bus in Mexico City and sat down. A few minutes later, the bus was in a terrible accident. As the bus cracked in two, some people were killed. A metal pole went through Frida's body. Her back was broken in three places. Other bones were broken, too. An ambulance rushed her to the hospital.

Frida was hurt so badly the doctors thought she would die. She spent a month in the hospital. From her neck to her hips, Frida was wrapped in a stiff cast.

17 de Septiembre de 1926 – FRIDA Kahlo (accidente)

A year after her accident, Frida drew this picture of the bus crash.

She could not move. After she went home, she still had to wear a cast and stay in bed for months.

To take her mind off her troubles, Frida started to paint. Her father brought brushes, paints, and canvas to her bedside. At first, she did portraits of her family and her friends. She painted the view outside her window and things in her room. Looking in a mirror hanging over her bed, she painted self-portraits— that is, pictures of herself.

After a few months, Frida could walk again. Her back would hurt for the rest of her life. But Frida was

At first Frida painted pictures of objects and scenes in her village. (The pictures here were part of a museum show in 2004.)

Self-Portrait in Velvet Dress, 1926, was Frida's first painting of herself.

stronger and braver than the pain. She would not let it spoil her life. Frida had another operation on her back in 1927. Again the doctor wrapped Frida's body in a stiff cast. Again she showed her feelings with brushes and paint. Frida used art to express more than she could say in words.

✳ 3 ✳

Frida and Diego

One day, when Frida was feeling better, she went to see Diego. He was busy working on a mural. She showed him three of her paintings. She wanted to know what he thought of her work. Was it good or not? Did she have any talent? Diego liked Frida's art. He said it was very good and told her to keep painting.

Diego began visiting Frida at her house. They talked about art and politics. They became good friends, and then they fell in love. On August 21, 1929, Frida married Diego. She was twenty-one years old. He was forty-one.

Frida began to dress in traditional Mexican clothes because Diego liked them. After a while, she

In this 1931 painting, *Frida and Diego Rivera*, Frida wears a long Mexican skirt and a shawl, called a *rebozo*.

Frida and Diego's wedding picture.

Luther Burbank

Frida tried a new way of painting in *Luther Burbank*, 1931. Luther Burbank worked with plants. Instead of showing how he really looked, Frida painted him as half man, and half tree.

became well known for wearing colorful clothes, lots of big jewelry, and interesting hairstyles. Some people said Frida made herself look like a work of art.

Diego was asked to paint some murals in the United States. In 1930 he and Frida went to San Francisco, California, and Diego painted two murals there. Frida and Diego were very popular. They went to parties at the homes of rich and important people.

Frida and Diego went back to Mexico in June 1931. Diego had a new house built for them. There were two parts connected by a bridge. One side was for Diego and his art studio. The other side was for Frida and her art studio.

In 1932 Frida and Diego traveled to Detroit, Michigan. The city was bustling with new factories. To Diego, it was very exciting. He painted murals showing workers making cars in a big factory. The next year, Frida and Diego went back to New York City for another of Diego's jobs. Frida made new friends and went to parties. She enjoyed shopping

Diego's house was pink. Frida's was blue.

and seeing movies. But most of all, she missed Mexico. She became more and more unhappy.

Frida was homesick for her family, for the foods and places of Mexico. Diego loved the United States. He liked the factories, machines, and noise of the cities. To Frida, the United States was a dirty place. The rich people were too rich, and the poor people were too poor.

Frida wanted to show her feelings about the United States. In *My Dress Hangs There*, she painted many of the things she did not like about America. An empty Mexican dress hangs in the middle of the painting: Frida wanted to go home.

Frida got her wish. In 1933 she and her husband went back to Mexico.

Here, Diego was working on the mural *Detroit Industry* at the Detroit Institute of Art.

My Dress Hangs There, 1933

Frida started this work in the United States and finished it in Mexico. This kind of picture is called a collage. Frida cut-and-pasted photos and other pictures, and she painted other parts.

❋ 4 ❋

Frida's Art

Back in Mexico, Frida continued to paint. Her artwork was very different from Diego's. While Diego mostly painted big murals on the walls of buildings, Frida made small paintings on wood or canvas. She also tried painting on metal, like the old Mexican *retablos*, which were small religious paintings on tin.

Diego painted in public places, with people watching. His pictures told stories, such as the history of Mexico. Frida painted at home, in private. Her art was very personal. It showed her feelings about her life. During her life, Frida painted fifty-five self-portraits. Sometimes she showed herself with

Frida loved animals. Her pet deer was named Granizo.

her pets. She had a baby deer, dogs, parrots, and monkeys. Her favorite was a spider monkey named Fulang-Chang.

Frida did not paint to please other people. She painted for herself and was happy to give her paintings away. She was surprised that other people liked her work.

An art gallery in New York City put on a special show of Frida's work in 1938, and she

Self-Portrait with Monkey Fulang-Chang, 1937.

The Frame, 1938, is painted on tin, like many old Mexican folk paintings.

sold a painting. It was her first sale. The next year, she had a show in Paris, France. The Louvre, a world-famous art museum in Paris, bought one of her self-portraits.

Frida's fame as an artist was growing. But she did not paint to make money or to become famous. Art was her way to express herself. Some people praised Frida for painting pictures of dreams and fantasies from her imagination. But Frida said they did not understand her work. "I never painted dreams," she said. "I painted my own reality." Her pictures showed how she saw herself and her world.

5

Becoming Famous

Frida and Diego loved each other, but they did not have a happy marriage. They often argued. In 1939, they divorced. Frida was very sad. To show how she felt about the end of her marriage, she painted *The Two Fridas*. In this picture, one of the Fridas has a broken heart. *The Two Fridas* became one of her best-known paintings.

Another painting after the divorce was *Self-Portrait with Cropped Hair*. In it, she wears a man's suit—not one of the colorful dresses Diego liked so much. She also cut off her beautiful long hair.

Frida works on her painting *The Two Fridas*.

Frida and Diego hated being apart. "This time has been the worst in my whole life," she said. They remarried on December 8, 1940. It was Diego's birthday. He was fifty-four years old.

Frida moved into her childhood home. It was painted bright blue and was called La Casa Azul (KAH-sah Ah-SOOL), which means the Blue House.

Self-Portrait with Cropped Hair, 1940.

Frida and Diego missed each other so much, they got married again.

In 1943 Frida began to teach at the School of Painting and Sculpture. Frida's students loved her. She took them on trips into Mexico City and taught them about Mexican history, too.

As Frida's health grew worse, it became hard for her to travel to the school. Instead, she invited the students to her house.

Frida had been in pain since the bus accident. It became even worse as she got older. She went to

Frida was known for her wonderful parties—cooking special dishes in her kitchen, above, and telling funny stories.

Frida in her bed.

many doctors. In 1950 she spent the whole year in the hospital, again painting from her bed. After more operations, she had to spend most of her time in a wheelchair.

Frida often sat here in this wheelchair to paint.

Frida's last paintings were mostly small pictures like this one: *Still Life with Fruit*, **1942.**

In April 1953, one of her best friends, a photographer named Lola Álvarez Bravo, put together a special show to honor Frida and her work. Frida was in terrible pain. Her doctors told her not to go out. But Frida refused to stay home. As the doors of the art gallery opened, an ambulance pulled up to the curb. There was Frida, dressed in her finest Mexican clothes and jewelry. The crowd went crazy.

Frida was carried inside. Her bed had been set up in the middle of the art gallery. Two hundred friends and fans gathered around her. Frida told jokes and stories. She and her friends sang Mexican songs until midnight. The night was very special for Frida.

Frida died on July 13, 1954, in La Casa Azul.

After her death, Diego gave the house and everything inside it to the Mexican people. La Casa Azul is now open to the public as the Frida Kahlo Museum.

Today, Frida Kahlo is known as one of Mexico's greatest painters. Her works of art hang in museums all over the world.

Frida was the first Latina to be honored on a U.S. stamp.

Frida's personal photos and notes can be seen at the Frida Kahlo Museum in Mexico City.

"I am happy to be alive as long as I can paint," said Frida.

⚜ Timeline ⚜

1907 Born in Coyoacán, Mexico, on July 6.

1913 Becomes ill with polio.

1925 Is badly hurt in a bus accident. Begins to paint while lying in bed.

1929 Marries Diego Rivera on August 21.

1938 Frida has an art show in New York City.

1939 Her art is shown in Paris, France. Frida and Diego get a divorce.

1940 They marry again on December 8.

1943 Begins teaching art at the School of Painting and Sculpture in Mexico City.

1953 Frida has her only art show in Mexico.

1954 She dies in La Casa Azul on July 13.

❋ Words to Know ❋

ambulance—A car for carrying people who are sick or hurt.

canvas—A strong cloth on which artists often paint.

divorce—To end a marriage.

fantasy—Something from the imagination.

mural—A huge painting on the walls of a building.

photographer—A person who takes pictures with a camera.

polio—A disease that attacks the muscles and makes it hard to walk. The disease is very rare today.

politics—The workings of the government.

preparatory—To get ready for something.
A preparatory school gets students ready for college.

reality—Something that is real, not imaginary.

self-portrait—An artist's picture of herself.

studio—A room where an artist works.

⁕ Learn More ⁕

Books

Frith, Margaret. *Frida Kahlo: The Artist Who Painted Herself*. New York: Grosset & Dunlap, 2003.

Holzhey, Magdalena. *Frida Kahlo: The Artist in the Blue House*. New York: Prestel Publishing, 2003.

Winter, Jonah. *Frida*. New York: Arthur Levine Books, 2002.

Internet Addresses

"Life and Times of Frida Kahlo" has information, photographs, and pictures of Frida's art.
<http://www.pbs.org/weta/fridakahlo>

A short bio and pictures of some of Frida's art.
<http://www.fridakahlo.com>

❊ Index ❊